SELF-EDIT YOUR NOVEL IN 8 STEPS

SELF-EDIT YOUR NOVEL IN 8 STEPS

BEAR AND GRIN IT

MARY ANN TIPPETT

MAT
BOOKS

The ability to simplify means to eliminate the unnecessary, so that the necessary may speak.

— HANS HOFMAN

BEAR & GRIN IT

This book is for all novelists looking to self-edit their first draft, inexpensively and systematically, into the best version possible.

While my method applies to all novelists, a "3 day novel" works well with this approach. Typically, novels written in three days are easier to whip into shape than those generated over longer periods. The reason relates to the writer's mindset. Intense focus produces more cohesive stories. More cohesive stories require fewer substantial changes.[1]

That said, every first draft is unique. Whether you wrote a novel in three days or three years, the action steps in this book will simplify your editing process. If you are staring down a finished manuscript, wondering where first to wield

---

1. For more on 3 day novel writing and how it works, buy *Write a Novel in 3 Days: The Zone Method* or download my free ebook, *3 Day Novel Writing: My Process, What Happens Each Day* at https://buymeacoffee.com/maryan ntip.

that red pen, this eight-step approach will bring clarity, determination, and peace of mind.

Ideally, you will BEAR the editing process with a GRIN on your face — which is why I organized my approach to editing around the BEAR & GRIN it acronym.

Here are the steps for self-editing your book into its best version:

1. Break Up
2. Edit Drunk
3. Assess Sober
4. Rewrite
5. Grammar Check
6. Remove Rubbish Words
7. Input-Gather
8. New Eyes

Don't worry. Alcohol is not strictly required in step two. We will get into the mental outlook required for a satisfying editing experience in due time. Just know that each phase shines a light on the essential attitude, tools and practicalities necessary for a solid editing experience.

I developed this method through trial and error. After self-editing eight of my books (and farming out the final polish for five of them) I learned from my mistakes, spotted some recurring editing themes, and eventually dispensed with bringing in professional editors for the final polish.

Since eliminating professional editors from the process, I've self-edited six novels, while also studying the editing processes honed by other authors.[2] Although key areas of my method reflect concepts that other guides touch upon, the eight-step process described here is easier to follow.

Many writing craft books illuminate one particular author's editing process, but few provide a simplified step-by-step format. Seeking clarity and a no-nonsense approach, I waded through dozens of succinctly written blogs and their wordier book-length cousins in order to develop a more straight-forward how-to guide on self-editing a novel.

The first half of the following steps may be a **bear** to get through, but you will be **grinning** by the last four. Let's get started on the BEAR & GRIN it approach to editing.

2. See "Recommended Reading" at the end of this book.

1

BREAK UP

"You can't start the next chapter if you keep reading the last one."

— Unknown

The first thing I do after writing a novel is break up with it. After typing "The End," creation mode is over. Like a bad first date, I walk away. I may have bonded with the story, formed a match in muse-heaven; but all good things must come to an end, beginning with my intense involvement with the first draft.

Do you have other story ideas? Now is the time to delve into one of those. Have you been dying to learn pickleball or quilting? Find a league or take lessons. Did you put a project on hold while you wrote the first draft? Now might be that project's moment to shine.

. . .

Run to a new project. Start a book club. Give your wardrobe an update. Reacquaint yourself with all those nice people you ignored while you were writing. Dive into the nitty-gritty of your day job. Whatever you do, don't be that person who shows up at their first draft's metaphorical front door to rehash the past. Time to let go, stand tall, gather some *new you* mojo, and slam the door on that first draft.

The reason for letting a novel rest is mindset. Breaking up with what you just wrote gives you time to heal, mature, and get to a place of objectivity. Before letting that draft back into your life, you need fresh eyes, a bird's-eye view, and a trace of mystery.

"You'll know you've let it sit long enough once you can pick up your draft and feel a little surprised at what's on the page," notes novelist Lira Samanta.[1] After getting to know your draft intimately, let yourself forget.

If you want a ballpark estimate of how long the breakup should last before laying eyes on your first draft, consider what other authors do. Matt Bell, author of New York Times Notable Book, *Appleseed*, lets his first drafts rest for at least six months.[2] Janice Hardy, award-winning fantasy author,

---

1. "How to Edit the First Draft of Your Novel," Lira Samanta, 2020, https://shutupwrite.com/articles/how-to-edit-the-first-draft-of-your-novel.
2. Matt Bell, *Refuse to Be Done: How to Write and Rewrite a Novel in Three Drafts* (Soho Press, Inc. 2022), p. 81.

suggests a few weeks.[3] Some authors advise writing a new novel before you edit the last one. However long you need to achieve the mental distance necessary to see your first draft with fresh eyes — this is your magic number.

Whether you fill that time working on something else, traveling, connecting with friends, or tackling that reading stack on your nightstand, you have one mission. Lose touch with the details of your story.

A great way to lose touch with your story is to move on to another one. When I write "the end" for one novel, I immediately focus on a new idea. Think of it like dating. Rebound relationships don't always work, but they serve a valuable purpose. They fill a void. Similarly, having a "work in progress" while a finished draft lurks in the background prevents the old manuscript from calling to you.

Putting aside the dating analogy for the moment, consider the money-making potential. Writing a new book while the last one rests means two books are in the works. The more books you publish, the more your capacity to earn expands. (More royalties, more eyes on your name, more opportunities to include "also by author" titles at the back of your books, etc.)

Another virtue of keeping one draft in the wings: "Dud"

---

3. Janice Hardy, *Revising Your Novel: First Draft to Finished Draft* (Janice Hardy, 2016), p. 320.

insurance. Not every book you write will be fixable. One advantage of editing in eight steps is the ability to nix an unsalvageable project. Not every first draft is a winner. Believe me, I have written some duds. The more time you put between your first draft and the next project, the better your ability to gauge its success. Do not let your excitement for the draft you just finished cloud your ability to judge it.

Okay, back to the dating analogy. Before I met the love of my life, I dated some duds. One (let's call him Garth) was a serial cheater. Another (let's call him Derek), after a disagreement, chose to keep his ego intact by refusing to drive me home. As I walked alone in the dark, I wondered, could I change Garth or Derek? If so, would the effort be worth it? Did their virtues outweigh their vices? No, no, and no. They were duds. Time to move on.

Love interests and first drafts have at least one thing in common. Sometimes you have to just walk away. No amount of time or distance can save it. Take, for example, my never-to-see-the-light-of-day story entitled *Love Actuary*. I hated to abandon the first draft of this holiday-themed romantic comedy that I planned to release around Christmas, but I had no choice. It was a dud. I loved the story when I wrote it. Not so much when editing it.

Misjudging a first draft happens. I pored over that Christmas story through six steps of editing, thinking I could fix it. When I arrived at the input-gathering stage, I received dismal news. The story bombed. None of my beta readers liked it. One even seemed put out for the time she spent reading it.

Could I have started over? Changed the dialogue? Created some intrigue? Maybe, but holiday books are meant to be jolly. Somehow, I had written a joyless holiday story. Rewriting it would have been an arduous, joy-sucking process. Like Garth and Derek, I turned my back on that deeply flawed experiment and opened myself up to new ideas.

Agonizing over the intrinsic flaws in that book, I decided, would waste precious time. Rewriting it would throw varnish on a dud. Instead, I turned to my "book ideas" folder, and pondered more promising options.

No one likes a breakup, but staying mired in a relationship that doesn't work is worse. When red flags pile up from one project, consider moving on.

The Three Months Rule

The rule of three is strong. Every book has three parts: a beginning, a middle, and an end. Musketeers, Magi, and the holy trinity are threesomes. The ancient Romans believed "everything that comes in threes is perfect."[4]

---

4. Aristotle, *Omne Trium Perfectum* (4th Century).

. . .

Three days lends itself to novel-writing because of the three-act structure: where you can devote one whole day to each main section of the book. The rule of three is a tidy, time-tested model. Leaving my manuscript alone for three months (or longer) works for me, which is why I recommend it.

After breaking up with a novel, I set my sights on a new idea. I research topics relevant to the next book, read books that are written in a style I want to imitate, and gather relevant information during the breakup period. (Did you notice the three actions in that sentence? Once you know the rule of three, you will see examples everywhere.)

Aim for leaving your first draft long enough to fall in love with another one. This can take anywhere from three to six months; sometimes longer, depending on travel, time of year, and social life. Three months, minimum, is my rule.

Contemplate the relevance of the breakup analogy for you. Think about the feelings associated with any exes in your life. Some may have taken years to get over. Others likely triggered an immediate good-riddance reaction. Either way, the same logic applies to your novel. Letting the details fade so a bigger picture can emerge will prepare you for the nitty-gritty mindset necessary for step two.

2

EDIT DRUNK

THE FIRST READ-THROUGH

"Wine is constant proof that God loves us and likes to see us happy."
— Benjamin Franklin

O kay, hear me out.

One of the most known pieces of writing advice, wrongly attributed to Ernest Hemingway, is "write drunk; edit sober."

.　.　.

I have tried writing while literally drunk. It does not work. Mostly, it leads to brain fog rather than clarity. Yet, writing "in the zone" can sometimes feel like a pleasantly buzzed experience. Never have I been more focused, more in the zone, more lost in the words flowing out of me than when my bottom was glued to a chair for three days of writing a complete book. Sometimes I feel loopy; once I actually hallucinated. This buzzed state can feel a lot like being drunk.

However, after writing six novels via the three-day-novel-writing method, I believe that loopy feeling is created by a brain that is hyper-focused on bringing your story through the trenches for a satisfying conclusion. Zone writing is a stone-cold-sober approach to completing a first draft. Therefore, I advocate writing sober, and editing drunk.

Let me explain.

When I picked up the first draft of *DoNut Enter* (my second cozy mystery) after letting it rest for several months, I did not like what I read. Every other word was trite. Typos and poor grammar glared. The voice was too prosy. Reading it brought on a sense of shame and disappointment. Deflated, I walked away for a few days and tried to steel myself for the most frustrating editing experience ever.

Then procrastination set in. Facing a disappointing draft you poured chunks of your life into produces a desperate feeling. You want to make it better, but dread the time it will take. You look for shortcuts. You will do anything to resurrect a terrible first draft from a destiny of pointlessness. This is the reality I faced when I stared down that disappointing first draft of *DoNut Enter*. Was it a dud? Would I have to breakup with that book for good?

Flash forward a few days. After a couple glasses of wine, I paused over that disappointing first draft while turning off my desk light. Thanks to an exceptional chardonnay, my mind was buzzing with openness and good cheer. Through wine goggles, I gazed upon that binder of printed pages and smiled sympathetically. Like a pilot spying a marooned sailor, I wanted to rescue it. Poor thing, I thought. It needs a saviour. With my new heroic mindset, I picked up that castaway draft and read a few lines.

Something strange happened. Instead of turning red with embarrassment over the haphazard sentences, my curiosity piqued. Was the *entire* manuscript bad, I wondered? Sometimes it takes me a few pages of writing to get a story off the ground. Perhaps if I kept reading, an interesting narrative would eventually shine through the lacklustre start.

Several pages in, my obsession over each word slipped away. Plot points I forgot I wrote took shape. Mentally, I patted my sad little tale on the head and said, "That's not a terrible story, Tippett. Nice job." This is how a potential dud came to life; by changing my mindset. Compassion enabled me to see a path through the woods.

. . .

This is the mindset you need when you pick up that manuscript for the first time after your very long breakup. You want to be in a happy place. You want to be in a patient place. If necessary, give yourself a pep talk first: something like, "it's time to give my story a life," or "let's dust off some dirt and find the diamond beneath." Maybe try a glass of buttery chardonnay. Or three.

Now read through your entire manuscript with no judgment. Get lost in the story. If an error or concern jumps out at you, make a quick notation in the margin or a notepad and move along. This is not the "major changes" part of editing. This is just you reading what you wrote and reacquainting yourself with the story. Try to enjoy this part. Producing a first draft took immense effort. Be proud of that and let the words carry you along the journey you spent countless hours mapping out.

If possible, set aside enough time to do this read-through with few or no breaks. When you are done, walk away for a day or two and let the continuity of the story gel in your mind. Maybe keep a notebook nearby in case you want to remember a theme or an intention that is taking shape in your mind. Consider whether you like the story in a "big picture" kind of way or whether its progression troubles you.

By the time you move on to the next step, you should feel bright-eyed and bushy-tailed. Your rose-coloured glasses are off. It's time to get real.

3

ASSESS SOBER

THE SECOND READ-THROUGH

"It does not matter how slowly you go as long as you do not
stop."
— Confucius

Full disclosure: I don't always enjoy editing. Some of
my books were easy to edit. Others needed more
TLC. I loathe the needy ones. Anticipating a high-
maintenance editing stint fills me with dread.

In the days leading up to my allotted editing time, the path to
my office might as well be a quagmire of weeds and muck.
Trudge, trudge, trudge. Will it be as good as I remember, I
wonder, as I sink one foot into the metaphorical mud? Will I

agonize over controversial parts? I worry, lifting my muck-covered boot, now ruined. Will I cringe over the awkward bits? I ask as I push a giant branch out of my way. How many sections will beg to be rearranged? I ponder, as the branch slips through my fingers and smacks me in the face.

These are time-consuming issues that I dread resolving: sensitive topics that might offend, cringy dialogue, misplaced plot points, sections of the story that belong somewhere else — the list goes on. I want my stories to behave from the start. Not all of them do.

What do you do when faced with a misbehaving first draft?

Ruthless Big-Picture Observation

When faced with a disobedient story, I employ some ground-rules. Like a new mom with a parenting handbook, I force myself to push through the methodical steps. For this second read-through, ruthless observation is the name of the game. This is where I walk past that tempting glass of wine and put on my big girl pants.

For the sober revision stage, there is no one-size-fits-all template. If the story flows logically and pleasantly, you can skip the "consider rewriting" chapter. All you need is what I call basic editing, a systematic clean-up process that requires less of a thorough analysis. If the story does not flow well, if it limps along with fits and starts, then rewriting may be the best place to start.

If you exceeded the number of words typical for your genre, you might focus on what to delete first. If your word count comes up short, you might look at manuscript lengthening strategies.

The point of this second read-through is to envision the big-picture issues. Decide if you can address them by inserting changes from the first read-through into the original document. If the answer is yes, open your document and do just that. Make corrections and insert changes from the notes you jotted down in the margins. After that, you are ready for the Grammar Check chapter.

If you feel overwhelmed after reviewing your notes from the first read-through, or if you sense the book has problems with structure, time line, plot holes, etc., consider rewriting rather than merely inserting changes into your original document. Look at the notes in your first draft's margins, along with any other notes you made while contemplating the story's themes, intentions, and cohesiveness. Make an honest assessment of whether you can improve the story with tweaks here and there rather than a massive overhaul.

Tweaks? Or Massive Overhaul?

. . .

The massive overhaul conclusion happened to me two times with salvageable books; five times if you count the drafts I abandoned.

The Shape of Us was a choppy story. I wrote it over a longer period than the others, which led to continuity problems. It didn't flow well, and some parts were annoyingly awkward. My goal for that book was to mimic what I call drugstore novels — those paperbacks you see near the magazines while you're picking up chips and bandaids. Drugstore novel covers are designed to captivate you with their escapist beach scenes and generically pleasing titles. Always keen to experiment, I wanted to write a book like that.

After working through some overwhelming feelings from step two (the drunk edit) of the editing process, I reread one of those drugstore novels and noticed how each chapter began with a sentence that summarized the ensuing chapter. Rather than tackling each tiny change the manuscript needed during the second read-through, I began with rewriting the novel with a summary-first approach in mind.

For each chapter I asked myself: What, essentially, was going to happen? Then I came up with a summarizing sentence to set the tone for what would occur in that chapter. "OF ALL THE SCENARIOS ANGELA HAD FRETTED OVER, BEING REJECTED WASN'T ONE OF THEM," I wrote at the start of Chapter 3, to set up the scene where a woman wanting weight loss tips was (almost) prevented from joining a meeting.

. . .

As I rewrote chapters, I dropped some details that did not work with the summarizing sentence and added more dialogue, description and action that worked with that summary's theme. Although I call it rewriting, the approach was methodical enough to keep me plowing through chapter after chapter.

The second major overhaul happened with *Write A Novel In 3 Days*. For that first draft, I spewed out a truckload of statistics and excerpts from my research. Then I looked at the unwieldy document and came up with a way to organize it through the ZONE acronym.[1] Once I had the structure in place, I plugged in relevant research points under their applicable sections that enabled the book to flow.

You should have a sense after your first (gentle, non-judgemental) read-through about whether your issues are primarily macro or micro. Big plot or structure problems versus tidying up language and grammar related problems. Overhaul versus tweaks. If moving forward seems too monumental, like moving mountains, you have a story in need of an overhaul; consider rewriting.

---

1. ZONE in and tune out.
   OUTLINE less.
   Nail the NECESSITIES.
   END your novel productively.

4

REWRITE

"Write. Rewrite. When not writing, read. I know of no shortcuts."
— Larry L. King

Rewriting sounds like a lot of work, but it is really just one way to add spice to your story. The first draft provides the bones of the book. The editing and revision stage is a chance to add some bells and whistles to the skeleton.

There are two ways to approach rewriting: come up with a structure for organizing the various pieces of the story; or tackle each chapter paragraph by paragraph, scene by scene.

Structure Approach

.   .   .

When I can think of a structure to frame the story around, I sleep better at night. *Write a Novel in 3 Days*, where I came up with the ZONE theory, is a good example. Once I had the acronym, (and it took some iterations to come up with one that worked), all the big ideas I wanted to share from research and experience found a place to live.

Pairs With Pinot is another example where structure brought cohesion to my story. Using a study that brought couples together by having them ask each other a list of questions, I began each chapter with one of those questions. Each chapter starts with a character's answer to a dating app question, revealing personality nuggets through their answers. The ensuing chapter for each question naturally flows from the kick-start each answer suggested.

Not all story ideas will lend themselves to a structural approach, but if you can think of one, this is an effective way to engage the reader and guide the plot points you want to address.

Paragraph By Paragraph Method

This method for rewriting a first draft breaks down the story into scenes. As I mentioned in the last chapter, *The Shape of Us* uses a version of the paragraph by paragraph approach. In that case, I looked at each chapter as a scene, asking myself what happens here? The answer to that question allowed me to introduce the chapter with a first sentence that foreshadowed the action ahead.

The book begins with: THERE WAS NOT ONE WEIGHT-LOSS OBSTACLE SUSAN SNOW COULD NOT SOLVE WITH A RECIPE. Writing that sentence followed from isolating the chapter's key plot points: 1) Susan's giftedness with recipe-creation; 2) Her frustration with a client who does not play by the rules; and 3) The introduction of a mirror with unusual properties. Those three plot points form a "scene."

To introduce the scene, I began with a sentence that summarized the first plot point. Then I moved on to Chapter Two and repeated the process: 1) Determine the plot points; and 2) Introduce those actions with a summarizing sentence.

There is a difference between tweaking your first draft and rewriting it. Starting each scene with a summarizing sentence assumes a scene clearly exists. If the first chapter's point eludes you, consider rewriting the chapter, or deleting it, or moving it to another place in the book — a massive overhaul. Tweaking each chapter may not be enough to save it.

Once you commit to rewriting, try to envision the book as a collection of scenes. Look at the story like a movie. Visualize the fading in and out of each scene that moves the plot forward cinematically. This way, you can sprinkle in dialogue, conflict, and action that movies employ to maintain interest.

. . .

Movie scenes break down into some of the following factors: (1) A character with a goal; (2) Conflict; (3) Antagonist; (4) Inner turmoil; (5) Problems or obstacles; (6) Actions; (7) Actions that lead to consequences; (8) Twists and unexpected events; (9) Tension and suspense; and (10) Dialogue.

You want the reader to keep reading. Readers have trouble putting a book down when conflict and tension lead them from one scene to the next. Each scene should have a purpose, preferably one that provides an incentive for the reader to keep reading. If there is no purpose or conflict in the scene, consider deleting it.

When forced to introduce a paragraph in one sentence, you will naturally draw out what action, conflict, and emotional engagement steps occur in the scene. When you move on to the next paragraph, one scene should lead to another when you summarize what happens there. Keeping the reader's attention is all about conflict, tension, goal, colourful characters, stirring images, and snappy dialogue. Your manuscript will improve instantly by zoning in on those key scene boosters.

Your goal is to delete the boring parts and insert excitement from scene to scene while rewriting your first draft.

5

GRAMMAR CHECK

"For your born writer, nothing is so healing as the realization
that he has come upon the right word."
— Catherine Drinker Bowen

Discovering the existence of grammar-checking programs was instrumental in my quest to avoid professional editing expenses. The one I chose allows me to spot and fix the biggest errors free-of-charge.

Once I figured out how to copy and paste scenes from my draft into a free version, my method came together. The software I use provides grammar, spelling and passive voice suggestions, among other things — services that expensive editors provide.

. . .

Why use a grammar-checking program over professional editing?

The Eighty Twenty Rule

If you are swimming in money, there is no reason to avoid professional editing. If you are determined to query your novel to agents and target traditional publishers, same answer. Professional editing can only help you put your best foot forward toward the querying process. Your only concern will be how to find an excellent editor.[1]

Before publishing my first book, I embraced professional editing options for two reasons:

1. All advice ever given to new novelists includes the importance of *the professional edit.* Good luck finding credible advice that says, "Your book will be fine without professional editing — it will sell like hotcakes, regardless;"
2. I wanted to avoid the embarrassment of publishing a novel full of errors. Thus, I hired a professional editor for my first book, *Clara & Pig,* and the next two books.

---

1. See "EDITORS I'VE WORKED WITH" at the end of this book, if you need a place to start.

Somewhere along the way, I realized that 99.9% of the time, authors do not make money by publishing **one** novel. They make money by publishing **multiple** novels.

The operative principle, known as the "80/20 Rule," suggests that 80% of results are produced by 20% of causes.

"80% of the results in a project may be achieved with 20% of the effort…80% of the satisfaction or happiness in one's life may come from 20% of their activities or relationships." [Medet Ali, Unlocking the Power of the 80/20 Rule: A Guide for Life and Success, LinkedIn.com (2023).]

This principle has various applications. For writing purposes, results (published novels) derive from writing related tasks. Therefore, I devote adequate time to writing related tasks such as idea-creation (thankfully, walking helps with this one), research, blogging, reading, editing, formatting and cover design. These tasks produce writing related results.

Once I understood how to complete a readable novel, my writing goal changed from "give your story a life" to "make a profit." From "holy moly, I finished a novel!" to "how do I make more money writing novels?"

Professional Editing Hurts Me More Than It Helps

.   .   .

For the first four novels, I tracked expenses and earnings. Royalties increased with each novel I published, but expenses eclipsed those earnings. Editing costs took a sizeable chunk away from earnings. Would I lose readers if my novels were riddled with errors? I wondered.

My fear of turning off readers because of errors that only a professional can catch evaporated when I learned two things: (1) Most readers who enjoy my books overlook small scale errors; and (2) Most published novels have small scale errors.

No matter how many manuscript read-throughs by professional editors, beta readers, and proof readers — even if you've had a thousand eyes on the document — mistakes get through.

Because I am an indie author, I control my books throughout the pre- and post-publication process. I can fix mistakes and upload revised manuscripts as often as necessary.

Have you spotted silly mistakes in traditionally published novels? I know I have. Usually, those mistakes are there to stay unless the book is successful enough to justify updated releases.

As a general rule, readers are more forgiving than I realized when the odd error pops up. If they like the story, if the book keeps them turning pages, a typo or grammar blip here and there will not sully their experience.

By book number five, I eliminated most of my third party expenses (formatting, cover design, and website maintenance) that were keeping me from a net profit. Editing costs were the last to go, because I bought into the writing advice that a professional edit is critical.

I discontinued professional editors after writing my sixth book. Having honed a system of my own, I concluded that self-editing is good enough. Instrumental to my approach is: 1) taking advantage of free grammar and style checkers; 2) knowing what to delete; 3) using beta readers; and 4) proofreading. Finally, my writing business was profitable!

Professional editing is a luxury service. If you can afford it, your book will probably improve from the process. If you cannot afford it, your book can still make money by following some important self-editing steps.

Grammar and Spell Check

This step, number five, in the self-editing process, is the easiest one. Go to the ProWritingAid website, bookmark it, and paste sections of your book into the Free Grammar Checker.[2]

Buying or subscribing to the software comes with useful enhancements. (With the free version, if you have brief chapters, you can probably copy and paste one chapter at a time, but too many pages may gum up the works, causing the program to stall. Or at least this used to be the case. The program worked seamlessly when I ran this book through the checker!)

My books are fairly short, requiring little more than one day for this step: copying and pasting a few pages at a time into the free grammar checker, and incorporating relevant changes the software suggests into my manuscript.

The process works like this:

1. After you breakup, drunk edit, soberly revise, and if necessary, rewrite your novel, print it and keep the hard copy at your side.
2. Open the free grammar checker and the most recent document version of your novel, and start plugging pages into the checker.
3. Wait a minute (or less) for the checker to do its thinking.
4. Then start at the beginning of the changes it

---

2. There are other grammar and spell checking programs out there. I am not promoting ProWritingAid. It's the first one I tried. So far, it works for me.

suggests and write them onto the hard copy at your side. (You can also toggle back and forth between the checker and your digital document to make these changes. I have used both approaches.)

Suggestions I typically receive from the checker relate to spelling, verb tense, passive voice, and other grammar rules. This step literally does what a copy editor would do. It's like having a professional editor in your back pocket!

When you finish this step, read your novel to ensure it makes sense with the changes you made from the grammar and spelling suggestions.

Voila! Instead of spending hundreds or thousands of dollars on an editor and waiting weeks or months for your improved manuscript, you will spend zero money and a day or two of your time.

Excited? Let's move on to the next step.

6

REMOVE RUBBISH WORDS

"The secret of being boring is to say everything."
— Voltaire

By now, you should have three versions of your manuscript:

1. The original draft.
2. The post revise-sober or rewritten draft.
3. And the post grammar-check draft.

With each version, you will have copied the entire draft of the latest version and pasted it into a new document, allowing you to make changes without losing the most recent version. For version four, you will be aiming to delete unnecessary words.

. . .

Personal Overuse Words

All authors struggle with words they tend to overuse. If you already know your overuse words, tackle them now, using the "Find" option (under "Edit" in the Pages software — it may be located elsewhere if you use Word or Scrivener).

You might overuse the words "that," "said," "sadly," or "good." Once you have self-edited a few times, you will learn which words form your Achilles heel.

One example of overuse words for me is starting sentences with "And" or "But."

One of my beta readers pointed out her dislike of sentences that begin with those two words. I commit this offence often. The occasional "and" or "but" at the beginning of a sentence might go unnoticed, but when you do it so often it becomes a pattern, readers are likely to pick up on it and be pulled from the story.

You want your reader's experience to be seamless. You do not want their attention to snag on repeated words. Thus, the first thing I do in search-and-destroy mode is look for ands and buts.

Rubbish Words

. . .

To give your house a cleaner appearance, you take out the trash. Similarly, to achieve the cleanest version of your story, you must eliminate rubbish words. Scan your document for the following throwaway words.

About, Actually, Again, Almost, Always, Anything, Appears, Approximately, At last, And then

Basically, Big

Close to

Else, Even, Enormous, Eventually, Every, Everything

Felt, Finally, Find

Giant, Great, Grin

Hard, Huge

Just, Just then

Kind of, Know

Large, Like, Little, Long, Look

Massive, Maybe, Merely, Mostly

Nearly, No, Nod

Of the, Of them, Oh, Once

Perhaps, Practically

Quite

Realize, Really

See, Seem, Seems, Shrug, Simply, Small, Smile, Soft, Somehow, Something, Sometimes, Somewhat, Sort of, Still, Strange, Strong, Suddenly, Surely

That, Then, Thick, Thin, Think, Thing, Tiny, Truly

Understand, Utterly

Vast, Very

Was, Watch, Weak, Weird, Well, Were, Wide, Wonder

Yes

. . .

As you search your document for rubbish words, in each case determine whether the sentence would be stronger if you delete the word or substitute a more precise one. You might conclude the sentence works best as is. In most cases, the story will improve from deleting or changing throwaway words.

Other Words To Cut

Besides personal overuse words and rubbish words, you will want to cut words from the categories below, especially if your word count exceeds the typical maximum for your genre. Using the grammar check tool from the last step will prompt you to incorporate most of these strategies for making a sentence stronger, but understanding why ProWritingAid uncovered a weak sentence will enable to you to spot more opportunities.

Here are some examples of issues often spotted in my writing:

- Adverbs: Especially those with "ly" endings. Do a find search for "ly" and ask yourself if a stronger verb will work. *They drove quickly* could be *they sped,* for example.
- Adjectives: Rather than using two or three, will one do? *Up ahead, the moody and serious*

mansion loomed might become *A brooding mansion appeared before us.*

- Words ending in "ing" or sentences featuring the word "was": To avoid passive sentences, consider rewriting *he was running* to *he ran,* and *it was assumed she left* to *we assumed she left.* Other words that signal a passive sentence are: were, by, and that.
- Repetitive information that could be one sentence. For example, "she filled him in on the details," might work better than repeating those details more than once.
- Unnecessary backstory. Backstory can slow down the reading. You want the reader to stay engaged.
- Speech tags. "He said / she said" speech tags typically go unnoticed by readers. However, consider strengthening them by substituting action words. *"The scone is delicious," she said,* becomes: *"The scone is delicious." She brushed a crumb from her lips.*

When To Add Words

What if you do such a bang-up job deleting unnecessary words that your page count falls short of genre expectations? Or what if you write first drafts in (ahem) three days, a strategy that notoriously produces novella sized books? In most cases, I solve this problem with the qué será será approach. If I read through the manuscript and feel it lacks nothing, and if my beta reader comments don't hint at missing parts to the story, I leave it alone.

With cozy mysteries and other books that feature food, you can add recipes at the end to prop up the word count. *Scone Cold Murder*, *The Shape of Us*, and *DoNut Enter* benefitted from this approach.

You might also consider adding an epilogue if you do not already have one. Beta readers of *Pairs With Pinot* wanted to know more about my happy rom-com couple. So I added an epilogue that brought most of the characters together a few weeks after the last scene.

You are the best judge of what might be missing in your novel and what you have too much of. That said, beta readers are your ace in the hole for spotting weaknesses (and strengths!) you overlook by being too close to the story.

7

INPUT GATHER

"Not to anticipate is already to moan."
— Leonardo da Vinci

The beta reading stage is the most important one. It is the ultimate chance to know for certain how your book will be received. Plus, the extra pairs of eyes on your writing can reveal editing issues that prior stages failed to illuminate.

Before the breakup, you and your book needed no input from the outside world. It was just the two of you, creating a hot mess of meaning from the spark of your idea.

The post breakup editing stage changes everything. Stripped bare of its misty-eyed newness, flaws in the story emerge. You dig deep and fix what you can, but your relationship with the original spark clouds your judgment. You need readers who have what you lack: objectivity.

Warts and all, your baby is ready for others to see. You are the parent hovering over a toddler, hanging onto its outstretched hands while it takes one step and then another into a whole different world. That world will see the story differently. That world will bring its own biases and sense of meaning to the words you wrote.

Before publication, I shared a snippet of *The Shape of Us* with a critique group. Someone commented that a character had "an eating disorder." They were not asking me whether that was my intention. They took what I wrote and assumed it as fact. Inside, I was fuming. How could they assume that? In my mind, the character's habits are the opposite of disordered eating.

That was a lightbulb moment for me. Once I publish a book, I realized, my reason for writing it flies out the window. Each reader will ascribe meaning to the themes, characters, and actions based on their vantage point, not mine.

I agonized over the decision to publish that book. I even brought my concerns to a Tarot card reader. (She is a good friend and helped me make a fun girls' night gathering around Tarot cards.) The feedback I received was, "It will be fine." It won't make a big splash, it won't fail. It will be okay.

.   .   .

Indeed, the book was fine. It did not strike gold, and it did not flop. Beta readers liked it. Some said it was my best work, and no negative reviews emerged. After putting to rest my temptation to scrap the book, I decided that sharing my message with the world mattered, even if the world missed my point.

The beta reading stage is your chance to get out of your own head. Making peace with possible outcomes ahead of time spares you regret and surprises. With enough input, you can anticipate how your book will be received. Knowing that "it will be fine" is better than imagining the worst-case scenario.

Publishing without beta input, however, is "already to moan," as da Vinci put it. Without beta readers, you might agonize endlessly over the way your novel might be perceived.

Knowing that actual readers found value in the book you wrote nips all of that moaning in the bud.

What Are Beta Readers?

Sometimes people confuse the term *beta readers* with the term *advanced reader copy* readers. Beta readers share some similarities with, but are different from, "ARC" readers.

.   .   .

Advanced Reader Copies of an author's final version of a novel are distributed to readers in order to garner feedback prior to publication. Traditional publishing houses use the ARC process to place a book in the hands of reviewers to create buzz and pre-release ratings.

Distributing beta reading copies, on the other hand, is a separate step that either precedes the ARC stage or replaces it.

Wikipedia defines a beta reader this way:

"A beta reader is a test reader of an unreleased work of literature or other writing who gives feedback from the point of view of an average reader to the author. A beta reader provides advice and comments in the opinions of an average reader. This feedback can be used by the writer to fix remaining issues with the plot, pacing, and consistency. The beta reader also serves as a sounding board to see if the book has had the intended intellectual and/or emotional impact on the target market." [https://en.wikipedia.org/wiki/Beta_reader]

At some point before publishing your novel, you need feedback from a typical reader. This stage might occur anywhere in the preceding steps; after the grammar check, for example, or even after the first one or two editing passes. When to solicit beta reader feedback will depend on your security about the story at any given stage. With my first book, *Clara & Pig*, I wanted to know if the story would have the same emotional impact on others as it did for me. For this reason, I engaged volunteers to read my story before I tackled any serious editing. Their responses gave me incentive to continue to the editing and pre-publication stages.

When I read *Scone Cold Murder,* my first cozy mystery, after the breakup phase, I did not feel comfortable with the book. It was a new genre for me, which clouded my judgment. When I mentioned to a friend that I might scrap the book and move on to a new idea, she asked to read it.

(A comment about friends and family: they are not ideal beta readers. They know you too well. Naturally biased, they sometimes see themselves in the characters or events. By knowing the author, they cannot be impartial.)

Since I did not solicit my friend's input, and had already planned to abandon the project, I decided her input couldn't hurt. I took her up on her offer and asked one other bookish friend to read it. What did I have to lose? To my surprise, both readers loved the book, which prompted me to invest time into editing it.

Since then, I have brought two other first drafts to these beta readers. In both cases, they disliked the story as much as I did.

. . .

My point here is that early beta readers can confirm or contradict your biased impression of your own work. Therefore, finding beta readers before you go to the trouble of self-editing is a step worth considering.

In most cases, however, beta readers should be called in later in the editing process. Self-editing gives you more confidence in your ability to predict whether a story works. This is why I recommend using beta readers after the biggest chunk of the editing process is done: after "search and destroy," and before "proofreading."

This is your last chance for uncovering any micro or macro issues the story might have, and the last opportunity to confirm that a story *you* think deserves publication will fly with the average reader.

How To Find Beta Readers

First, a summary of my experience. For book one, *Clara & Pig*, I swapped manuscripts with another writer I met through a meet-up group in my city. We agreed to exchange manuscripts and share feedback with each other.

For book two, I asked my very busy friend with a career in journalism (who I try not to bother) for her opinion. She pointed out an important omission I would have missed: requesting permission from the author of the study I used in my book to reference his work. In addition to that valuable feedback, I received accolades from her that provided the confidence I needed to publish.

For book three, I paid an expert to edit, format, design the cover and coach me on marketing options. From that process, I learned about sensitivity readers, which prompted me to reach out to a friend who knew more about the belief system I wrote about in that book. After his feedback assuring me that what I wrote about that belief system was not offensive, I felt comfortable skipping the beta reading stage.

By the fourth book, I had a network of writers on Instagram who liked my writing style and were willing to read and review my books. The beta reader search became easier with each published book. Anywhere from three to seven readers usually respond to my plea for volunteers.

No matter where you find your beta readers, know they are as important in the editing process as grammar checking and proofreading. Without them, you walk into the publishing arena blind.

Questions For Beta Readers

Ideally, when you give the most recent version of your novel to volunteer beta readers, you will include some additional questions.

. . .

What to ask beta readers depends on the book and your specific concerns. My questions vary from book to book, although my primary focus is whether the first page makes the reader want to read on, whether there were any parts of the story that dragged, and whether the ending was satisfying.[1]

For my most recent book, *One Day*, I gave this list of questions to beta readers:

- What did you take away as the major theme of the book?
- Did the plot make sense to you? Which part of the book made you not want to put it down?
- Where (if anywhere) did you feel the transition from one chapter to the next was too "jarring" (leaving you feeling as though you may have missed something)?
- Do the first 5 pages make you want to keep reading? If not, why did you lose interest?

---

1. The following resources will give you a place to start for developing your own list of questions:

    https://thejohnfox.com/2022/06/essential-questions-to-ask-your-beta-readers/

    https://writingcooperative.com/15-questions-to-send-beta-first-readers-please-steal-3ff9fa198b5

    https://stacyclaflin.com/beta-reader-questionnaire/

    https://s3.nybookeditors.com/blog/PDF/Beta-Reader-Questionnaire.pdf?mtime=20190822225536&focal=none

    https://authority.pub/questions-for-beta-readers/

- Did you feel yourself losing interest at any point?
- Who was your favourite character?
- Is there a relationship or situation you would like for me to have explored more in depth?
- Was the dialogue believable?
- Was there any point where it wasn't believable or required more than average focus to read through?
- Did you notice any discrepancies in time, places, characters, or other details?
- What do you think are the weakest two chapters? What do they seem to be missing?
- Did you find the ending emotionally fulfilling?
- How would you describe this book to someone else?

Keep in mind that for every beta reader who dislikes your story is one who loves it. Their role is opinion-based. Opinions are, by nature, biased.

Approach the beta reading process with a take-it-or-leave-it mentality. Use the feedback to understand how your story *might* be perceived. Be grateful for comments that enable you to fix something you missed, or to clarify something you did not notice was fuzzy, or for highlighting places you could enhance the story's impact (such as adding an epilogue, for example).

You have to be happy with your story. Beta readers can help you feel happier about it.

8

NEW EYES

"I do my best proofreading when I hit send."
— Unknown

A fter you incorporate suggestions raised by your beta readers into the final draft, you need a proof-reader to catch errors missed during the seven steps, particularly mistakes that sneak in while incorporating beta reader suggestions.

You can find lots of advice on proofreading if you look hard enough. One of my favourites (that I do not use) is to read each sentence of your novel backwards as a final proof-reading effort. Theoretically, this method forces the content to appear out of context, where you are more likely to notice errors that escaped your attention after reading something multiple times. Good advice, I admit, but tedious.

. . .

To ensure the best results, find a friend who is well suited for such a task and have them proofread your final draft. Desirable character traits for this job include:

1. Interest in you as an author;
2. Meticulous nature; and
3. Bribable with food or coffee.

I have used two such people. One is a schoolteacher who actually enjoys these types of tasks and is not only thorough but also quite charming and nice about it. The other is my husband, who admittedly has better things to do than proofread my work and probably doesn't enjoy it that much. He is meticulous and judgmental and sometimes inserts humorous comments in his corrections. ("How many times can you write the word novel?" he commented while proofreading my book about novel-writing.)

Neither of these people are professional proofreaders. Like authors editing a first draft, they miss a few errors, but they do have the luxury of experiencing the story for the first time. They are called in the last minute to do what I can no longer do: review something that I've combed through at least eight times as if it's new. They are the last set of fresh eyes on the manuscript.

After you correct mistakes pointed out from proofreading, this is the end. Your editing journey is done! Savour it. Make yourself a special treat. Do a happy dance. Whatever it takes to let this sink in: You made it through the hardest part.

The BREAKUP.
> The drunk EDIT.
> The sober ASSESSMENT.
> The REWRITE.
> The GRAMMAR check.
> The RUBBISH words removal.
> The INPUT-GATHERING.
> The NEW EYES final review.

Maybe you powered through it like a BEAR collecting berries. Maybe you pasted a GRIN on your face to make the process less arduous. Maybe you BEARLY tolerated checking off the steps. Maybe your GRIN morphed into maniacal laughter when error after error popped up, despite your best efforts to quash them.

But you finished. Your book is in a better place than it was before you began the self-editing process. It may not be perfect, but perfection is overrated.

A FINAL WORD

My goal for this book was to provide for others what I was looking for in a self-editing guide. I wanted to write a simple, easy to follow book on how to self-edit a novel. Was the path to that accomplishment easy? Probably not. Weirdly, I barely remember the difficult parts now.

I aimed to share what I have learned about editing novels. I conducted some research. I focused on my own methods, made sense of other authors' advice, and sketched out the details one step at a time.

Hopefully, I removed some of the mystique around self-editing. My best advice, if I can pin it down to one major tenet, is to tackle your project with the proper mindset.

Jump into the abyss and start swimming, just like you did when you finished that novel. Use this book as your map. No more flailing about in fits of euphoria and despair. Just swim toward that first step. After that, set your sights on step two. Then keep swimming.

Some day, I may write a book on self-publishing. Although such an endeavour is outside the scope of this title, you will find some rudimentary concepts that frame my publishing journey after this final chapter. Whether you opt to self-publish or query traditional publishers, some of these tips apply to both paths.

To guide you, I am also including actual notes from editing my most recent book. This is the first time I transformed my experience into a play-by-play of each step. If it is unhelpful, skip it. Otherwise, gather what bits interest you from the process and discard the rest.

I am also including a list of books I found enlightening as I crafted my method of self-editing. The not-so-helpful ones shall go unmentioned.

Lastly, I am providing a short list of professional editors who, in one form or another, made a difference in my writerly journey. Just in case you prefer to bring in the big guns.

Now you have all you need to edit your masterpiece. When you publish your book, give me a shout. I cannot wait to see what you can do!

SOME SELF-PUBLISHING TIPS

Why Choose The Indie-Publishing Route?

I have never seriously considered pursuing the traditional publishing route. From what I have learned and observed, the process would be soul-crushing for me.

By the time I reached a point in life where I could indulge my dream of writing a novel, I wanted to check off that bucket list item and give my story a life. The chances of being traditionally published are not in an aspiring author's favour. For me, barking up that tree felt like a useless waste of time.

As it happens, I enjoy learning how to tackle each step in the self-publishing process: cover design; editing; formatting; positioning a book among a myriad of genre options; marketing; and most importantly, how to accomplish these steps without going broke.

. . .

The ins and outs of the indie book scene change from year to year. Personally, I use three publishing platforms to upload my books to the relevant sales channels. Last year, one of the platforms absorbed another that I once used. Another platform is more expensive and less intuitive than the others.

My best advice is to start with one platform, then add other platforms as they become accessible. Because of the occasional fluctuations among platforms, I cannot offer reliable advice on how to navigate that side of the indie publishing process.

Primarily, my tips address how to save money through indie publishing. I hope that sharing where I made my mistakes will spare you from doing the same. If your goal is to make a profit from writing books, I suggest focusing on the following strategies.

Build Relationships

When I finally had the time and opportunity to focus on novel writing, I sought out writing groups in my community. The Ottawa Writers Circle had a strong presence — organizing write-in sessions at public places like malls and food courts, bringing in established authors and writing experts to speak on key topics, and arranging meeting opportunities at restaurants and pubs for writers to get to know each other and form friendships. It was a great way to get advice from seasoned writers and commiserate about writing related issues.

. . .

Later, I found a Writing Workshop at my local library that meets one evening each month. An author who began as an indie publisher leads the workshop, and eventually broke into the traditional publishing world. We sit around a group of tables and take turns sharing our work. The leader usually gives everyone a chance to share, after which other participants critique the writing submissions. For me, this has been a good way to build up the courage to share my work with others. It also gave me a model for critiquing various kinds of writing.

Meanwhile, I started an Instagram profile for my author persona. Through that platform, I connected with other authors, writers, and readers. Some of us organized a peer review group, where we would read, rate and review each others' books. This method has been instrumental in getting my books in front of other readers, gathering feedback, and developing a following for readers who enjoy my work.

I joined Twitter (now X). There too I connected with other readers and writers. Primarily through these social networks, I learned to market myself and my work by engaging with others authentically, and sharing my thoughts on books that I read as posts and videos. Using the hashtag #writingcommunity is a good way to access other X users who dabble in or make money from writing.

. . .

Choose two social media platforms for growing an audience. Facebook and TikTok are additional forums where writers gather, but choosing just one or two places to post is a more efficient use of time. Growing followers and relationships takes time and effort, but your primary focus is to write. Fewer social media outlets enable you to hone your marketing strategies and preserve that precious writing time.

Think about what interests you and what you can offer the writing and/or reading community. I try to add value by blogging and vlogging about books I read. In the beginning, I set up a website for my reviews, and linked the website to my Instagram and Twitter pages. I changed websites a couple of times, and ultimately determined that maintaining a website costs more money than it is worth. Eventually, I found buymeacoffee.com, which is free and allows people who enjoy your writing to "buy you a coffee," or sponsor you. This has been a much better fit for me.

Besides blogging about books, I began blogging about book clubs to learn more about them and to amass material for a how-to book. I also blog about writing and publishing tips as they come up. In this way, my website provides searchable information for people who value my opinion on reading and for people seeking guidance on writing.

I also post a video review once a week on books I finish reading. This started when I read a book that excited me so much, I wanted to share it with others. It took me awhile to hone my casual vlog style, but this once per week video draws more interactions than my other posts. All to say, if you find something you are good at and/or excited about, make that the thing that will help you find your audience and make connections.

To build your community, write blogs or book reviews. Support other authors with shout-outs, critiques, ratings and reviews on Goodreads, Amazon, Bookbub, etc.

Find a platform for sharing those pieces of writing, preferably for free. Consider opting for a free blogging platform like WordPress or Buy Me A Coffee. Find reviewers willing to swap or provide honest reviews without compensation.

Podcasts

Learning from other authors and writers is instrumental in the publishing process. Writing related podcasts I enjoy are: The Creative Penn ("TCP"); The Shit No One Tells You About Writing ("TSNOTYAW"); and Story Nerd ("SN").

TCP provides information on how to support yourself as an indie author. It also features guests from the indie publishing world who speak about new technologies and tricks of the trade. TSNOTYAW showcases literary agents critiquing traditional publishing query letters (in mostly the women's fiction genre). SN is a square-off between two movie buffs who discuss a different movie in each episode. They pick apart each movie's strengths and weaknesses from a story-telling perspective.

. . .

These are just a few of the thousands of podcasts out there that illuminate the job of writing. Find a podcast or two that resonates with you. This is a great way to learn about the writing lifestyle and how to hone your writing and editing process.

Become An Expert In Publishing Tasks

As I mentioned before, novel writing was a losing proposition for me until I learned to eliminate expenses. Once I learned how to design covers, format manuscripts for uploading to publishing platforms, and edit, my only real expense became buying my own paperbacks to keep on hand for local bookstores to sell. Achieving a net loss of almost zero in my business came from listening to podcasts and trying out options.

Book Covers

Stock cover designs are relatively inexpensive, as low as $200. I am picky about covers, because everyone judges books by their covers.

Although you might find good cover artists on freelance-related websites, I found designers by word of mouth or by noting the cover artist on jackets of attractive novels.

Three of my covers cost close to $1000 each. I got lucky with another two covers, when a graphic designer I met on Instagram offered a $100 per cover deal. Despite this excellent deal, spending $100 for cover art was enough to eclipse my earnings.

Then I discovered a graphic design app for editing photos and videos. I had been using it to design my Instagram posts, so I could make my page look consistent and attractive. The app's ebook feature allows me to design covers that I can upload on platforms that offer paperback cover conversion options. One platform has a cover creator on their publishing platform that will accept an ebook cover I create on the design app, and turn it into a paperback cover.

One of the platform's paperback design features never works for me, and another I find overly complicated. Some day, either I will figure out what I need to learn to make these platforms work, or they will simplify the uploading process.

One downside of the graphic design app I use is that it saves its best designs for people who upgrade to the premium level. That said, the extra searching I have to do to find adequate designs, and the extra efforts I make to alter cover concepts in order to adapt to the non-premium designs, are worthwhile endeavours to keep publishing costs low.

Editing

You are well on your way to saving another enormous expense by reading this book. Editing for my novella sized books once cost me between $200 and $1,000. I would be a bankrupt author if I'd continued paying for covers and editing, which I now consider luxury services.

Formatting

Vellum is a program that charges a fee to download. For that onetime cost, you get all upgrades for free. The program provides several types of formatting from which to choose.

Before I discovered Vellum (a formatting software for MACs), I paid $200 or more to format each book. Trusting someone else with the formatting means relying on their availability to reformat when errors are found or the cover design changes. Vellum's one-time fee is $200-300, depending on which iteration you use. I paid the lower amount and have since that time formatted six books this way.

Had I continued paying for this service for each book, I would be in the hole for at least $1,200 by now. If you plan to publish many books and often, Vellum is well worth the investment. (Atticus is the PC version of Vellum and seems to garner rave reviews.)

Gather Your Tribe

Making my writing life public was not a comfortable move for me, but I realized early on that stepping out of my comfort zone eventually produces fans of my writing. It also attracts other writers and members from both creative and practical communities.

Gather your tribe. Celebrate successes with friends and family, organize a book signing at a pub or bookstore when your book reaches a certain number of sales, reviews, or conquers some other measurable goal.

Indie bookstores are often willing to facilitate book signings. Explore your options and attend author and book events in your area. Maybe even pitch a book idea at a writing conference out of town. The more you put yourself out there, the more of a community you will assemble.

REAL-TIME NOTES FROM EDITING

ACTUAL NOTES FROM TAKING ONE OF MY BOOKS THROUGH THE 8-STEP PROCESS

As I was working on SELF-EDIT YOUR NOVEL: 8 STEPS, the time came for editing the novella I wrote during the 2022 3-Day Novel Writing Contest. What follows are my notes from self-editing *One Day* f/k/a *Pound Job Day*. This realistic snap-shot, of specific issues that may occur during the eight steps, demonstrates how I resolved them.[1]

I. BREAKUP PERIOD — almost a year from the writing first draft (10-20 months). Wrote the book in September, 2022. Started editing in July, 2023.

II. DRUNK EDIT

---

1. I made very few changes from the literal notes I scratched onto the manuscript during the editing process here, which makes for unexciting reading. The intent is to show the bare bones process without any bells and whistles.

- Change title — One Day? Today Again? Today? (Originally, I thought "pound job day" would evoke "ground hog day" vibes. Since the book repeats the same day like the movie "Groundhog Day," and because the main character is constantly trying to get to Saturday when she volunteers at the rescue — "or pound." I thought it was a clever title. But upon reflection, the title Pound Job Day falls flat. I needed a title that pulls the reader in. Since other popular books have been called "One Day," and the term hints at the theme of only having one day to "get it right," I ultimately went with this title.)
- Simplify wordy sentences.
- Should Stella have a make-over scene?
- Should inner thoughts be italicized?
- Scene setting (River and canal form a loop? Dad's issue — "you have to"?)
- Better names for river and canal.
- Not sure about town name. Need a theme.
- Strike out wordy sentences and make them clearer.
- Name of café: Bridge Cafe?
- What's the boss of a publishing company called? Title?
- <u>Thoughts</u>: 1st chapter ends well but I gotta say this was a slog. Maybe I don't have the right mindset. :(Think I'll do chapter two after a drink!

❄

- After Happy Hour lunch, 2 glasses of wine…

- Day One — Chapter 2 better. Writing has a certain rhythm I just let wash over me. Still some things to work out. Terms to rename. Dialogue to tighten, etc. But as a reader, I want to see what happens next!
- After a weekend of fun, drinking and shenanigans...
- Day Two — Need a last name for Stella. More action beats. Momentum of the story is feeling slightly better now.
- Day Three — Dialogue needs action tags in places, but otherwise better. God story needs simplification, show not tell, specify religion? Or leave out God part. Just about church in general. Chapter's end makes me want to keep reading.
- Day Four — Better writing in this chapter too, but needs some improvements.
- Day Five — Writing was almost flawless. Had to keep reading! <u>Love the ending</u> but needs an epilogue. Before moving on to next step, I'll reacquaint myself with how other authors dealt with each stage, and the endings. See where I can elaborate, etc.
- Need to possibly rewrite the first few chapters to make ending even more satisfying.
- Other thoughts: POV? (I was wondering if I should stick with present tense or change to past tense, for example.) Why does dad prefer canal? Rename river and canal. Rename town? What's the theme/message to convey with the setting? Constellations? Navigation?

III. SOBER ASSESSMENT

- Decided to incorporate changes from notes, clarifying first chapter and making it stronger. (This stage took over a week, working a few hours at a time each day. Started with leaving the house so I could focus, then just continuing the momentum, bit by bit each day.)
- Not sure if I need an epilogue. Will ask beta readers what they think of ending. (After I put a call out for beta readers on social media, I jotted down the names of volunteers and their email information and file format preference at the top corner of my notes.)

IV. GRAMMAR CHECK

p. 6 (I checked off pages that I ran through the grammar checker, copying and pasting the draft sections into the software program, one to three pages at a time.)

p. 7, p. 11-15, p. 16-20, p. 21-24, p. 25-29, p. 30-33, p. 34-37, p. 38-41, p. 42-45, p.46-49, p. 50-53, p. 54-57, p.58-61, p. 62-64

(Grammar checking 64 pages took about 3 hours.)

V. SEARCH & DESTROY

I skipped this step because grammar check picked up weak words. But I used the find function to reconcile inconsistencies in spelling of the town Oakville. Also skipped rewrite step, pending feedback from beta readers.

VI. BETA READERS

I came up with four volunteers from one Instagram Post and Story. Once I had four confirmed, I stopped searching because this is the perfect number and because I felt confident all four would follow through on their commitment. As it turns out, one of the volunteers did not complete the task, but I never followed up with him because I received plenty of useful feedback from the remaining three. (Ideally, one should seek out seven beta readers and count on at least three backing out. But I have a history with these particular volunteers that reassured me.)

While waiting for beta feedback, I worked on some pre-publication tasks:

- Book formatting (I uploaded the draft to Vellum, even though I knew it would not be the final version, so that I could provide a variety of pleasing-to-the-eye file-format reading options for beta readers).
- Draft of Acknowledgments, bio, and epilogue considerations.
- Draft of Author's Note: why I wrote this book, and suggestions for other day-repeating books I recommend (a Christmas one, The Re-Do, etc.)
- Apply for ISBN numbers
- Comparative pricing research
- Key words for Amazon, etc. plus researching potential genres and sub-genres of similarly themed books for when it's time to upload the book to the publishing platform(s)

VII. INCORPORATING BETA INPUT

- Make Stella younger (I planned to make her older, but as the story unfolded, she needed to be younger than her boss), age 29, 8 years as assistant editor.
- Take out reference to Minerva being old.
- Add descriptions for Cal, Stella, Minerva & Kyle so reader can picture them.
- Today Chapter: add description of bedroom and kitchen as well as neighbor Margot's room plan to show how the two apartments are laid out.
- p. 30 Kim scene is confusing? (This input led me to realize that a huge chunk of the book from a late chapter had been omitted, which explained why the beta reader was confused by that part. This was a huge, huge help! Thankfully, I saved a hard copy of the original printout. Otherwise, that chunk of the story would need to have been recreated from scratch.)*
- I had literally reread the MS from start to finish, adding description and fixing errors I somehow missed before, which is how I figured out what the beta reader's confusion was. Re-reading (so time consuming!) was key — a necessary step!
- *Learned from another beta reader she only got 35 of the 70 pages. No idea how that happened. Luckily, three out of the four betas had not read their copies yet, so I was able to apologize and send the full versions to them without causing them too much extra work.
- Lesson learned: Check in with betas after a week. Ensure their version is okay. (words, chapters, pages, etc.)!

- Once again, figured out a whole chapter (Day Two) was missing. Had to re-send to beta readers again!
- Received feedback from beta one: not her type of book.
- Feedback from beta two: Felt let down by ending, but loved it from the beginning; Today chapter, sentence 2: "The scent of maple and butter though, that's different." (one sentence instead of two); p. 4, par 4, sentence 2: "window," not "widow;" p. 8, par 3, sent 2: Unclear if river or gap sounds like a long exhale (STET); P. 10, last par, sent 3: steed to keep "moving," not "move," or omit "keep;" p.14,1st par, last sent: delete sentence (confusing); Day One chapter, par 2: consider not specifying date (decided to reject this idea); p. 30, last par: Before leaving "the office" with Kim, instead of "the firm;" end of Day Three chapter, last par, says "I have a saucy romance..." as last sentence. Did she get fired? Has another chunk of the novel gone missing? (Answer: No. That's how I wrote it. Consider adding something about the firing?); Day Four chapter, p. 53, par 2: comma after "money;" Next sentence: "We have plans today" needs quotation marks; Day Five chapter, p. 60, par 5: change firm to office; par 7: "Minerva" should be Stella; par 8: change "allowing" to allow and delete "at;" sentence 2: change "her" to "Minerva." Ending: would love to see her discover this is Saturday and that she lived the perfect Friday to see Saturday. And maybe she looks forward to Monday to start her new journey. (My own note: Maybe Trevor calls her at home?

Depending on what happened the day before.
Maybe Stella asks brother to help with shelter?
Maybe we see dad making plans with Margot? —
Decided to keep the ending as is.)

- After working on blurb, I took another look at last
chapter. A.I. (Chat GBT) gave me helpful ideas on
blurb, but terrible results on satisfying endings.
Saw an article online that spoke to elements of
perfect endings. Considerations: transformation;
suspense and surprise. After rereading my last
chapter, I realized that instead of leaving things
open to interpretation as intended, I left things
unresolved. So I added a sentence that gave a
bigger hint at the resolution, with an element of
surprise. (Publishing hint: A.I. can be helpful.
Scanning articles on the internet can also help,
such as how to end a novel.)

VIII. FINAL PROOFREADING

The following notes were generated by a proofreader's
comments on the final draft.

- Reminder to self: change "trap" to "capture" in
prologue.
- He didn't have title or prologue. Suggested "to"
for "he will be catching a flight (to) somewhere
interesting."
- Because I gave him a pdf without the Vellum
formatting, he wondered why Today chapter
wasn't "Day One," etc. (This helped to remind me
to fix chapter headings in Vellum when I upload
the proofed version.)

- Questioned spelling of boss's (I was right).
- Questioned whether "riffling" should be "rifling." Because rifling denotes sinister motives, I stuck with riffling.
- Added hyphen to "football-like" build.
- Suggested "high-grade" for coffee rather than "top notch." I left it as top notch.
- (He didn't catch this, but I noticed another error while reviewing his comments (comma where a period should be). How many other errors got missed, I wondered.
- Noticed a plural verb that should be singular.
- Questioned a comma that ProWritingAid had me put in. I'll stick with PWA.
- Caught a noun that should be plural.
- Caught a pagination error.
- Noted "looking" used twice in one sentence. Re-worded one of them.
- Suggested "repetitious" instead of "day-repeating" loop. Good idea.
- Caught an improperly placed "a" in a sentence.
- Suggested Bravo for Brava. I'm right, but I double-checked.
- Flagged "sub genre," so I added a hyphen. Can't hurt.
- Noticed a "will" that should be "with."

After incorporating Proofreader's comments, I created documents for <u>Afterword</u>, <u>Acknowledgments</u>, <u>About Author</u>, and <u>Also By</u> and added these to the Vellum document. Then I "generated" new document files (for ePub, pdf, and mobi), and double-checked all versions for these additions.

RECOMMENDED READING

Over the years, while honing my own self-editing process, I appreciated the advice shared from the following writing guides (in order of most helpful):

Gwen Hayes, *Romancing the Beat: Story Structure for Romance Novels* (Gwen Hayes, 2016)

Matt Bell, *Refuse to be Done: How to Write and Rewrite a Novel in Three Drafts* (Soho Press, Inc. 2022)

Thomas Emson, *How to Write a Novel in 6 Months* (Thomas Emson, 2013, 2020)

Becky Clark, *Eight Weeks to a Complete Novel: Write Faster, Write Better, Be More Organized* (Becky Clark, 2020)

Kathy Stewart, *Self-Editing Your Novel: An Editor's Tips to Make Your Work Shine* (Authors' Ally, 2014)

RECOMMENDED READING

Janice Hardy, *Revising Your Novel: First Draft to Finished Draft* (Janice Hardy, 2016)

RECOMMENDED EDITORS

If you conclude you are not ready for self-editing and/or prefer to use a professional editor at any stage in the writing or editing process, I can recommend the following fabulous editors.

Rob Bignell, the most reasonably priced and efficient editor of the bunch, who provided copyediting services for two of my books.

Website: **http://www.inventingrealityediting.com**
LinkedIn: Rob Bignell, Editor
Instagram: @inventingrealityeditingservice

Chris Wheary, line and copy editor who specializes in the romance genre.

Website: **https://cmwheary.com/**
LinkedIn: Christine Wheary
Instagram: @cmwhearyediting

April Bamburg, who provides line and copyediting, and proofreading services. She once rescued a blog post I was working on from a host of embarrassing errors.

Website: **https://www.writingunfiltered.com/**
LinkedIn: April Bamburg, Writing Unfiltered
Instagram: @writingunfiltered
Email: **april@writingunfiltered.com**

Brenna Bailey, one of the more pleasant and encouraging copy editors I have worked with who helped usher two of my books into the world.

Website: **https://www.bookmarteneditorial.com/**
LinkedIn: Brenna Bailey-Davies, Bookmarten Editorial
Instagram: @bookmarteneditorial
Email: **contact@bookmarteneditorial.com**

Jennifer Milius, developmental editor and author stylist who also interviews fascinating creators on her podcast, TufFish.

Website: **https://www.jennifermilius.com/**
LinkedIn: Jennifer Milius
Instagram: @authorjennifermilius

ACKNOWLEDGMENTS

For the following people who helped make this self-help book happen, I am eternally grateful:

The Beta Reading Gang — Carole Moran, Cathy Quigg, and Sara Daniels. These three bestowed much needed clarity, insight and organization to the chapter titles and their content.

Alan — proofreader virtuoso. (When I can catch him between bike rides.)

Every friend and family member who casually asked, "What are you working on now?" which nudged me closer to finishing. How many times can I answer that question without boring these people, who don't write or edit novels, to tears?

Most importantly, YOU, the reader! Thank you for picking up this book and for deeming it worthy of your time.

ABOUT THE AUTHOR

Mary Ann Tippett is the author of eight novels and two writing craft books. When she is not writing or reading, she is blogging about writing and reading on buymeacoffe.com/maryanntip. She lives in Ottawa with her outdoorsy husband and her sock obsessed schnoodle.

𝕏 ⓘ ♪

ALSO BY MARY ANN TIPPETT

Write a Novel in 3 Days

Food For Writers

Pairs With Pinot

The Shape of Us

Clara & Pig

Finding Clara

Scone Cold Murder

DoNut Enter

One Day

Christmas Getaway (Coming Soon!)

www.ingramcontent.com/pod-product-compliance
Lightning Source LLC
Chambersburg PA
CBHW071246020426
42333CB00015B/1645